Zero Fucks

The 21st Century Man's Guide to Deep Self-Confidence

Avery G. Hayden

Contents

Introduction: What Is the Zero Fucks Given?

Chapter 1: Zero Fucks Given

Chapter 2: The Uncanny Power of Mindset

Chapter 3: The Meaning Problem

Chapter 4: The Unexpected Cause of All Your Insecurities

Chapter 5: Nature Versus Nurture

Chapter 6: The Nurturing of a Shitty Self-Image

Chapter 7: The False Assumption That Ruins Men's Dating Lives

Chapter 8: Embrace Social Tension

Chapter 9: Opportunity Over Risk

Chapter 10: Embrace Your Flaws

Chapter 11: On Surrender

Chapter 12: Kill Complaint

Chapter 13: An Outward Focus

Conclusion: It's Not All About You

What Is Zero Fucks Given?

This is a book about self-confidence. *Zero Fucks Given* won't teach you the words that will make you sound confident, the body language that will make you appear confident, or the visualization exercises that will make you feel confident. *Zero Fucks Given* will teach you how to become confident.

Self-confidence isn't a quality that can be forced. The harder you try to appear confident, the less confident others will perceive you to be. You've seen the guys who try a little too hard: to be dominant, to look as if they're in charge, to act like they don't care what others think. In truth, these efforts are all symptoms of insecurity.

Most self-improvement advice feeds on and magnifies our insecurities: the techniques they teach us only serve to make us more self-conscious. While you try to open up your body language to look dominant, you are actively reminding yourself that you don't feel dominant enough to begin with.

Trying to be confident is much like trying to be funny. If someone says to you, "Make me laugh," What happens? Because you're on the spot, you try to force humor. It doesn't work. Even if the words you say are funny, the words lose their power because you are trying too hard.

To build deep self-confidence: genuine confidence that attracts respect and admiration from others, you must understand that trying to appear confident is a doomed strategy. The more you try to appear confident, the more attention you will bring to your insecurities, which will in turn, make you feel insecure.

What other approach is there? How can you become more confident without trying to look more confident? First, you must become aware of the insecurities that you don't know you have. As soon as you become aware of these negative beliefs that are holding you back, you will be empowered to free yourself from them.

Secondly, you must get comfortable with making yourself emotionally vulnerable. You must take social risks that make you feel uncomfortable, through this, you will develop the emotional callouses of groundedness and self-belief. To do this, you will need to change your relationship with negative emotions; the following pages will show you how to accomplish exactly that.

The pages in this book will teach you a psychologically sound approach to developing confidence that isn't based on appearances, but on core self-belief. You will learn to care less about what others think, and in so doing, make others think more positively of you. You will learn to stop trying to be something, and in so doing, become the person that others desperately try to be.

Make no mistake, this isn't an easy process. I'm not offering a panacea that will solve all your social difficulties without effort. Instead, you're going to learn how to invest your efforts in a way that produces worthwhile results.

This book isn't going to give you a hit of validation by telling you how awesome you are; and it's not designed to give you a false sense of accomplishment simply by reading its pages. Instead, it will give you the real, no-bullshit insights that helped me transition from one of the most socially insecure people I know, to one of the most self-confident.

The following chapters contain an amalgam of concepts drawn from both scientific sources and personal experience. These pages are like a map and a compass, pointing you in the right direction. Without your own efforts, they are meaningless, but when used as tools, they can catalyze deep self-confidence.

This journey begins by looking at what self-confidence is, and what it is not.

Chapter 1: Zero Fucks Given

The archetype of self-confidence that inspires the most driven (and sometimes desperate) imitation, is the guy who gives zero fucks. This is for good reason:

The guy who gives zero fucks is the guy other men want to be and women want to be with; everything he does disproportionately draws the attention of others.

People imitate him not because he's perfect, but because he's comfortable with his imperfections. Women want to be with him not because he's unusually attractive, but because he doesn't worry that women might not find him attractive. Others believe in him not because he's unusually skilled, but because he believes in himself.

Other people call him confident, charismatic, and charming, not because he has some measurable quality that others don't, but because everything he does reflects how little he worries about others' opinions. Some people hate him, but he doesn't waste his time, energy, or emotions on those people.

We all secretly envy what we falsely assume is his innate social superiority to others.

I'm Jack's Need to Belong

Tyler Durden from Fight Club is the cultural icon for giving zero fucks. He genuinely did not care what anyone else thought, and because of this, he had no desire to be nice, appropriate, or agreeable.

He laughed at what most people feared, and he was so unafraid of social rejection, and so at ease with his own imperfections that people admired him, even worshiped him.

Even though he is a fictional character that ran underground fight clubs (sorry for talking about it, but to be fair, everyone breaks the first rule), his character was so magnetically appealing that real people started actual fight clubs based on the movie. Eight years after the movie's release, a fight club got started at my high school due to my best friend's admiration for Tyler Durden and what he represented.

And what did this sociopathic cult-leader who didn't care about anything, including himself, represent? He put it best himself. When speaking to the narrator of the movie he said, "All the ways you wish you could be, that's me. I am smart, capable, and most importantly, I am free in all the ways you are not."

Tyler Durden became a cultural icon because he represented total social and personal freedom, a freedom most of us envy, because deep down, we know we don't have it. We care too fucking much about the opinion of others.

Throughout our childhood and adolescence, we were inundated with bullshit beliefs and values that taught us what is important and how we should act. Naturally, we've accepted these beliefs as our own. We were fed these ideologies in our formative years; to abandon these beliefs now would put us at war with ourselves. Let's expose the bullshit that is unconsciously choking our ability to interact with others as our most genuine and charismatic selves.

We've all known a few of those guys who just don't care what other people think, and secretly or not, we wish we had what they have. There's nothing terribly special about these guys who are envied. They just have a mindset that allows them to have deep confidence in themselves.

The Uncanny Power of Mindset

Most self-improvement advice focuses on external qualities and outward behaviors. This makes sense, the external is all we can observe. If you want to be more charismatic, a book might teach you how to make good eye contact, change the tone of voice that you speak with, or use a power-pose to exude confidence.

There is some truth to this flavor of advice. Strong eye contact and open body language do show confidence. But, having put many years and thousands of hours of conscious effort into a medley of these techniques and 'tricks' to build confidence, I can say they're not very effective, and that they even entirely miss the point.

There are severe limitations to this popular brand of practical advice. First, in the process of learning these kinds of techniques, you're going to appear, and even feel less confident. The very act of monitoring your body language to match an ideal you want to emulate, is bringing your attention to the fact that you don't like your body language, and that you need to fix it to come across as confident.

But there's an even worse limitation to this kind of advice. We attribute charisma and confidence to their external symptoms. Things we can see, like someone's body language, how a person talks, how they listen, and their eye contact. But what really makes them different isn't something you can see, it's something that is completely invisible: it's their mindset.

The lens someone with deep confidence sees the world through is qualitatively different than the lens most people see the world through. It's because of this lens that these people naturally act in visibly more confident ways. External traits like word choice, body language, and the quality of your voice are the tip of the iceberg; they're the 1% of confidence that you can see with your eyes, but the vast majority of what makes people who are deeply self-confident different is what lies beneath the surface. These external attributes are the symptoms of confidence, your mindset is the cause.

Do you think people who are extremely self-confident- who don't give a fuck what anyone else thinks- are worried about their body language or the tone of their voice? No. They don't even consider things like this as worthy of their attention. They are so confident because they don't monitor themselves, because they don't feel their external behaviors are lacking in any way. They believe they're already good enough, and because of this, they act in ways that appear confident.

Scientific research on mindsets has found that a simple mindset intervention can make changes that last a lifetime. In one groundbreaking study, psychologist Jeremy Jamieson tested the power of mindset. He split college students into two groups (the study was controlled for GPA and SAT scores) and gave the first group a mindset intervention to change their beliefs about test anxiety before having them take a practice version of a standardized test.

The mindset intervention was a simple lecture in which Jamieson showed students evidence that test anxiety isn't fundamentally bad. And that, in fact, research has shown high stress-levels can improve performance. Therefore, Jamieson said, you shouldn't resist test anxiety, you should embrace it, because it can actually help you.

Jamieson hoped that this message would boost students' performance, and it did. Students in the mindset intervention group of the study performed significantly better on the practice test than the other students who received no lecture.

That's right, simply being told that test anxiety is a good thing improved students' actual scores.

If you're thinking, "Maybe the mindset intervention made the students feel less stressed about the test, and that's why they did better," it's a good thought; that's why Jamieson took saliva samples immediately before students took the practice test.

Students who received the mindset intervention had higher levels of salivary alpha-amylase than those who did not, meaning they had a stronger physical stress response to taking the test. Despite this, their performance was superior to the control group who did not receive a mindset intervention and experienced less stress when taking the test.

Over the next several months, these same students took the actual GRE, and sent their scores to Jamieson's team. What Jamieson found here was even more surprising than the results of the initial study. Students who received the mindset intervention (months earlier) did better on the GRE than those who did not, and the difference in scores was *larger* than it had been with the practice test, thus implying that the effect had grown stronger over time.

I know this sounds too good to be true. I thought the same thing when I first learned about mindset interventions, but Jamieson's study is only one of hundreds that have demonstrated the uncanny power of mindset.

In another study, researcher Alia Crum found that a simple five-minute mindset intervention in which she told maids that housework is a great way to burn calories was shockingly effective. The maids who received the mindset intervention reduced their body fat percentage and blood pressure significantly in a course of only eight weeks. This is compared to a second group of housemaids who did not receive a mindset intervention experienced an increase in body fat percentage and blood pressure in the same period of time.

The best explanation for this strange result, is that, when the maids were told that their work was actually a great form of exercise, they unconsciously worked harder, and thus, got in better shape; all because of a simple five-minute mindset interaction.

In a 1998 study, 30,000 American adults were asked how much stress they experienced the past year and whether they believed stress was harmful. Unsurprisingly, those who reported a high amount of stress over the past year, and believed that stress was harmful, had a higher chance of dying over the next eight years: 43 percent higher chance, to be exact.

Unexpectedly, though, those surveyed who believed stress was not harmful were less likely to die over the next eight years than any group who believed that stress was harmful. For example, those who had high levels of stress, but believed stress was not harmful, were less likely to die than those who experienced low levels of stress, but believed that stress was harmful. Therefore, your mindset about stress affects the physical impact that stress has on you, to the point where it significantly affects your chance of dying over the next eight years.

This is just scratching the surface of mindset research, but mindset studies have consistently found that meaningful, lasting change can be facilitated through a simple mindset intervention that takes as few as five minutes to complete. Psychologists have found, time and again, that our real-world outcomes are determined by unconscious mindsets: beliefs that in many cases, we aren't even aware we have.

Most people have mindsets that cause them to act in unconfident and neurotic ways. You're not afraid to approach a girl because you didn't do a power pose to boost your confidence. You're afraid to approach a girl because of beliefs you have about yourself that feel real, simply because you've had them for years.

Change your belief systems, and the rest will take care of itself over time. This doesn't mean change is easy; it takes a lot of honest self-reflection and requires you to develop an ability to question your most deeply rooted assumptions about what social interactions mean.

The Meaning Problem

We care too much about what people think of us because we think their opinion of us *means* something. When getting rejected by that girl means something to you, for example, you're going to experience intense emotions which make that rejection feel like it matters.

To some other guy, though, dating that girl doesn't mean anything. It's just something he'd like to do. Without hesitation, he makes a move and ends up dating her. To him it wasn't a big deal. The more meaning an interaction or person has to you, the more power you give them over you.

How Meaning Becomes Emotion

When I was 18 years old my father died suddenly. He was my closest friend and personal hero. The loss hit me hard. One day, several months after his death, I was playing drums and I started to feel a numb sensation in my left arm. I paused for a second, and thought to myself, "That's weird, didn't I hear somewhere that your left arm goes numb when you're having a heart attack?"

I brushed the thought off and went back to the song, but the thought kept creeping back, and I noticed that my arm was growing number. This built up, moment by moment, and I began to drown in the feeling that something terrible was about to happen. I was about to have a heart attack.

I stopped playing, dropped my sticks, and started feeling notably lightheaded and dizzy. I was losing control. Breathing was becoming increasingly difficult. I was suffocating. Time was running out. I stumbled towards my room, holding my arm against the wall to keep me steady. I got onto my computer and looked up heart attack symptoms.

> Difficulty breathing: Check.

> Dizziness: Check.

> Numbness in the left arm: Check.

> Sense of impending doom: Check.

I had every symptom listed on the page. I went from worrying that I might have a heart attack to being certain that I was having one at that very moment. I woke my mom up in her room and told her that I needed an ambulance because I was having a heart attack. She was bewildered for a moment, and then said, "Have you heard of a panic attack?"

Hours later, I still hadn't calmed down, so I found myself in an urgent care. Through a variety of tests, I learned that my symptoms didn't mean what I thought they meant. What I so recently knew they meant. What had happened was entirely a creation of my own mind, it was a result of the meaning I had attributed to an odd sensation in my left arm.

As soon as I started to think that the numbness in my left arm meant I was having a heart attack, the thought took a life of its own, and my mind started searching for evidence that I might be dying.

The human mind has an incredible ability to find (and even create) evidence that something it's looking for is occurring in objective reality. My brain focused on, and exaggerated, the sensations I was feeling. It put my body into fight-or-flight mode, and then interpreted my fight-or-flight symptoms as further evidence that I was indeed having a heart attack.

It's an insidious self-fulfilling prophecy. We look for evidence that our interpretation of the meaning of an event is accurate, and then our brain misinterprets external events as proof that our interpretation was correct.

You've probably felt similarly weird bodily sensations many times, but you didn't give those feelings any meaning, you didn't care about them. As a result, you didn't have a panic attack. The numbness in my left arm had a significant meaning to me (created by a fear of dying suddenly like my father had), therefore, I created an anxiety disorder.

Our social lives follow a similar pattern, we give meaning to whether someone laughs at our jokes, we give meaning to asking a girl out, we give meaning to our social reputation, and that meaning creates very real negative emotions. That discomfort we experience when we want to express ourselves feels totally real, and it creates a self-fulfilling prophecy. We fear that people won't like us if we vulnerably express ourselves, and so, we hold our tongue whenever we have an opportunity to be vulnerable. Then, because we didn't express ourselves genuinely, people don't get the opportunity to connect with our real personality: and they end up liking us less.

 To change the meaning you give to social interactions, you must learn what stories you're telling yourself that make you feel less confident than you could.

15

The Unexpected Cause of All Your Insecurities

If there is one thing that weighs us down in our social (and professional) lives, it is caring about what other people think of us. In fact, it's easy to observe how so many people become their own worst enemy by caring too much.

You can clearly see that your friend cares so much about whether his crush likes him back that he won't even ask her out. You can tell that your other friend is afraid to be free-spirited, and puts on a serious front because he's afraid that people won't approve of his genuine, goofy personality.

But can you see similar behaviors in yourself? Probably not. It's not the flaws that you are aware of that cause insecurity and self-esteem issues. It's the flaws you're not aware of, the self-defeating beliefs you don't even know you have.

Nobel Prize winner and author of *Thinking, Fast and Slow*, Daniel Kahneman, explains this problem brilliantly, "We're blind to our blindness. We have very little idea of how little we know. We're not designed to know how little we know."

The harsh truth is that your analysis of what's causing your social problems is inaccurate, limited, and completely biased. If you want to make a change, you must first learn the true cause of your social problems; understanding this is the foundation that any social self-improvement must be built on.

Self-confidence and charisma are largely the results of a virtuous self-fulfilling prophecy. Psychologists have found that social expectations become social outcomes. This has been shown time and again by research on a powerful psychological force known as the Pygmalion Effect.

Imagine a babysitter is warned by a friend that the kid she's going to babysit is a real shithead; he's impatient, annoying, and arrogant. After hearing this, the babysitter becomes anxious about meeting this kid.

When she finally meets him, just as expected, he's horrible. This kid won't listen to her, he has a short temper, and he treats her with total contempt.

There's something the babysitter was totally blind to. The kid she babysat wasn't usually a shithead, he was usually a perfectly normal kid. He acted like a shithead because she expected him to act like a shithead. Psychologists believe this happens because when we expect people to act a certain way, we treat them differently (often without our awareness). The person that's a total asshole around you, might be a saint around someone else.

This matches common sense. If, for example, you were a Trump supporter and you met Hillary Clinton, you'd probably treat her very differently than a supporter of hers would, and she would probably treat you differently than she would treat a supporter of hers.

We don't just cause people to treat us differently based on our expectations of how they will act; our negative beliefs about ourselves cause other people to treat us differently too. If you don't respect yourself, your behavior will reflect this (and people will treat you with less respect).

Someone who is self-pitying gets pity, not respect. If you believe you're a social pariah who doesn't deserve to be liked, you're going to act uncomfortably around people. You will be shy and closed off. This behavior will repel people. As you notice that people don't seem to like you, you're going to perceive this as even more evidence that you are, in fact, a weirdo who doesn't deserve to be liked. Then, you're going to act even more shy and closed-off around others, and this pattern will repeat itself as a negative spiral, ad nauseam.

If we were aware this was happening, it would be easy enough to deal with. But we usually aren't. We only live in our own mind which can easily become a vacuum chamber of negative, self-defeating beliefs. We can't understand how a better mindset would change our life for a similar reason that a deaf person can't really understand how hearing would change theirs.

Unless we become aware of the possibility that our mindset is damaging, and is negative in ways that it doesn't need to be, we don't have the proper context to understand how our mindset is affecting us. A lack of this awareness causes you to think that it's not your behavior that's repelling people, but that it's the 'fact' that you're a weirdo or inherently flawed that's repelling people.

Without knowing it, we become our own worst enemy. We might believe people are assholes, but we don't realize they're just reflecting our own beliefs back at us. We might believe we're not worthy of affection, but we don't realize that we wall ourselves off from vulnerability and make it impossible to receive affection. We might believe we don't deserve a girlfriend, but we don't realize that we could easily get a girlfriend if we just took the right actions.

In countless ways, we fuck ourselves. Our brain is constantly looking for an explanation for our problems, and we blame those problems on something we don't think we can control to free ourselves of responsibility. We do this because it's easy.

Like it or not, your brain is designed to take the easy route, and facing insecurities is never easy. The truth is that you are in control of (and therefore responsible) for all your social shortcomings, but it's intrinsically difficult to notice the damage you're doing to yourself.

Changing yourself isn't hard because it takes so much willpower or hard work. Change is hard because it requires openminded introspection and honest questioning of your own thoughts, behaviors, and values.

Case Study: A Man Who Fucked Himself Over Without Knowing it

I had a friend, Brandon, who was an interesting case. Brandon was good looking by societal standards, 6'2, blonde hair, blue eyes, athletic build. He generally seemed socially confident. You would never guess that he had a crippling anxiety towards meeting women.

He had hooked up with a number of women by getting wasted and trolling the bars, but they were rarely the kind of women he wanted in his life. Still, he would take what he could get and often date the first girl who would sleep with him. Once, he even dated a girl he wasn't sexually attracted to for an entire year.

After a few years of this drunken debauchery, he met a girl who actually met his standards; she was athletic, ambitious, confident, caring, and everyone loved her. He was extremely nervous when he met her, but with some nudging from his friends, he managed to go on a few dates with her. After they started dating, he began acting incredibly neurotic.

Because of his nerves about this dream girl of his, he decided he needed to meet other women to get his mind off of her. He found a girl on tinder, slept with her, then on the same day (while the tinder girl was still at our house), invited his dream girl to come by. She came over, and the situation quickly deteriorated into sitcom-level awkwardness because Brandon told his dream girl that he had slept with this other girl from Tinder. Unsurprisingly, this turned the girl he really liked off, and they stopped dating.

A couple months later, Brandon met his dream girl again. He was afraid to approach her, but another friend and I convinced him to do it. Surprisingly, she was happy to see him and they made plans to hang out again. Brandon never followed through with these plans.

Brandon hasn't slept with another girl in six months since this happened. He will declare that he needs to start meeting women again, and he'll go out once or twice (for 30 minutes before he drives back home); but then he'll say he needs to focus on his career before getting back to dating.

Recently (months after this all happened), Brandon realized he was intentionally self-sabotaging his relationship with his dream girl. According to him, she fucked him up. He said what happened made him unable to meet women anymore, that he was scarred, and this is why he won't go out.

From the outside looking in, Brandon's behavior is clearly neurotic. But to him, it all made logical sense. That's the real problem, it's so obvious how other people unnecessarily fuck themselves over, but we all have a bias to be blind to our own similar behavior. It's easy to notice when someone else is falling into a neurotic, self-destructive pattern, but it's incredibly difficult to admit that you're doing this to yourself.

Brandon's mindset has a foundational issue that's preventing him from growing. He is dealing with his relationship problems using what psychologists call a static mindset. A static mindset is a belief that people don't change, that we are victim to our external circumstances. A static mindset is a ruthless self-fulfilling prophecy.

For example, you can have a static belief that you aren't intelligent. Maybe you didn't excel in school early on and the feedback you got made you believe that school just isn't for you, that you just aren't smart enough. Over time, this calcified into a static mindset that said you are not smart; that you, as a person, aren't able to be a good student. This mindset becomes self-reinforcing.

If you have this mindset, when you are assigned homework, you tell yourself that you're not smart enough to be a good student, so you avoid the homework or approach it halfheartedly. When you read for class, you don't pay attention, because, what's the point? You're not going to get anything out of it anyway, school's just a waste of time for a dumb kid like you.

Then the grades come in, your parents are disappointed, and this negative feedback is stressful. The easiest way to interpret this feedback is to blame your failure on something outside of your control. Something essential to who you are, like your lack of intelligence.

By doing this, you relieve yourself from the pain of knowing that your own decisions are causing you to fail. By doing this, it's not your fault. Instead, it's like a disease, something you don't have to blame yourself for, something that you're a victim to.

This is a self-belief that can only lead to negative feelings about yourself. Sure, you alleviate yourself from responsibility for your problems, but you accomplished this through negative self-evaluation. This frees you from one source of stress, and traps you in another, far more damning stress: the feeling of helplessness. You paralyze yourself and make action impossible, because your mindset says action is pointless, that you're not good enough, no matter what you do.

Brandon believes that he doesn't deserve a healthy relationship based on mutual respect. So, he makes it impossible for himself to get in this kind of relationship. He avoids meeting women unless he gets wasted, and when he does meet a woman he really likes, he self-sabotages the relationship in such a way that it's doomed to end before it ever really began.

He tells himself a story about why this is happening, a story about who he is: a person that is fundamentally damaged, wounded, a victim. And through making himself a victim, he entitles himself to continue acting in self-destructive ways. He self-sabotages his relationships by making ridiculous decisions like inviting his dream girl over while he was on a date with a random Tinder girl.

And those self-destructive behaviors reinforce his static, negative self-beliefs. He must be damaged or he wouldn't keep acting in such self-harming ways. If he weren't a victim, then why does he keep making the same mistakes without ever escaping the cycle? Most people do this. The differentiator between those who change and those who do not is how effective they are at becoming aware of the damage they're doing to themselves

Every time you catch yourself falling into a self-destructive social pattern, you are opening yourself up to change. This is the only way to make real, substantial, growth. Ask yourself how you might be doing this to yourself right now. It may be mild, it may be extreme, but self-destructive patterns are there. No one's mindset is perfectly enlightened. We all have negative beliefs about ourselves. The path towards deep social confidence is a path of building awareness of the many ways in which your mindset is damaging you; this allows you to finally be free to let go of and disprove them.

Don't think of your mindset as something you need to 'fix', in a paradoxical way, this gives that mindset more charge, more power. What you resist, persists. Actively fighting against a mindset is emotionally acknowledging that mindset as valid. Conscious rebellion doesn't work, the path towards true change is counterintuitive: it is surrender.

By accepting you do have negative self-beliefs, by surrendering to the fact that these mindsets are affecting you, they lose their emotional power over you. This is the path to freeing yourself from self-imposed limitations.

Nature Versus Nurture

"But I'm an introvert. This stuff doesn't apply to me."

As long as you believe that your nature is harming you in some way, it will. You're giving yourself a logical excuse to avoid changing your behaviors. You can't change your results if you don't give yourself permission to try.

Whatever quality you think is holding back, whether it be introversion, a lack of social intelligence, or social anxiety, that quality is partially within your control. Not entirely, but you have enough power to change it that using it as an excuse only robs you of authority over your own life.

In the scientific community, the nature versus nurture debate is over. The consensus is that it's nature and nurture. Twin studies have shown that personality traits (like introversion) are generally between 30 and 60 percent heritable. This leaves sufficient room for you to overcome any innate disadvantages you may have.

Recent neurological research has found that the brain is far more adaptable to long-term change than we ever could have previously imagined. The brain can adapt to any new situation; for example, research has shown that when introverted people act like extroverts, they start to feel happier.

This implies that the fact that extroverted people enjoy social interaction more than introverts may not be due to their inherent differences, but due to the fact that acting extroverted inherently feels good. Introverts have a natural tendency to be shy and unassertive, but they can reap the benefits of extroversion by learning it like a skill. Even if by default you are shy or socially anxious, you can make a point to act as an extrovert, and in so doing, feel like an extrovert.

Perceived Status

The neurotransmitter serotonin is a feel-good chemical: too little serotonin is associated with depression. You might be surprised to learn that your baseline levels of serotonin can be changed without a chemical intervention.

Research has shown that when someone's social status is increased (by being promoted in their fraternity, for example: Mcguire 1983), their baseline levels of serotonin also increases. The brain adapts to higher social-status by actually changing your brain chemistry.

Robert Wright, author of the acclaimed evolutionary psychology book, The Moral Animal writes, "Serotonin levels, though a "biological" thing, is largely a product of the social environment. It isn't nature's way of destining people at birth for leadership; it's nature's way of equipping them for leadership once they've gotten there."

This doesn't mean you need to join a frat and get promoted to become more extroverted and socially confident. It means that your perception of your social status can actually change how you feel and behave.

How do you do this? The first step, is of course, to act extroverted. The more you keep to yourself, hold back your tongue, and avoid social interaction, the more you're able to judge yourself and make negative assumptions. If you act like you have low status, you will feel like you are low status.

Someone with high-status would feel comfortable meeting strangers, a CEO wouldn't feel nervous to meet his employees; it's the employees who are nervous to meet the CEO. To adapt this mindset, you must behave like you have high-status first, then you can reap the benefits of a perceived status increase.

I've experienced this effect myself. At the beginning of a night when I go to a bar or a club, I do not want to meet strangers. I would much prefer to just go back home. But because I know that if I start interacting with people, I will start to feel like an extrovert (and therefore, will enjoy socializing), I push through the initial resistance, and within ten to twenty minutes I'm in a social, fun mood.

Over time, this process has become easier to go through. Over the years, my nerves at the beginning of a night out have decreased from severe to mild. Each night I act extroverted, my bias to feel shy and anxious decreases just a bit more. Maybe, genetically, I still have a bias to be introverted, but no one would ever guess that, because I've changed my personality through building extroversion as a skill.

Years ago, I was diagnosed with anxiety. A psychiatrist told me I would be anxious forever. I never saw that psychiatrist again. I wasn't going to accept the notion that anxiety was something beyond my control. I was going to overcome it, no matter what it took.

I tried a variety of different strategies to overcome my anxiety, and most fell flat of my expectations. Except one. When I made a habit of acting in ways that someone with social anxiety normally wouldn't (meeting people at bars, asking girls on dates, etc..) my anxiety started to subside.

Over the months, my anxiety progressively lessened until it reached a point where I had less social anxiety than the average person. Considering that six years ago, I would get panic attacks just from going to a public location (like a mall), I'd define that as noteworthy progress.

I knew my anxiety had power over me, I wasn't delusional; it was a very real limitation. What I didn't believe was that my anxiety was insurmountable. I believed that my inherent limitation didn't have to be a permanent limitation. If social interaction is painful for you, you're not confident, or you're unable to get a date, you can change this. The first crucial step is to be open to the idea that it's possible, and the second is to take assertive actions.

The Nurturing of a Shitty Self-Image

Your self-image is a biased, inaccurate, collection of beliefs that were created by external influences. These beliefs were formed when you were too young to filter out the relentless deluge of bullshit that we are all exposed to, day in and day out. Your parents, teachers, peers, and media influences planted the seeds of the mindset that you now carry with you.

Remember the movie Inception? In that movie, an inception was an event in which a team planted an idea in someone's dream that would take root and change their life without their knowledge. They would think the incepted belief was their own idea because it came to them from a dream.

You probably haven't had your dreams hijacked, but we have all been influenced by a psychological force eerily similar to an inception. When you were a child and your parents angrily told you not to talk back, your school taught you to shut up and listen, and commercials taught you that you needed a new product to feel good about yourself, you were too young and vulnerable to distinguish these ideas as toxic. You were a sponge absorbing everything around you.

At your current age, you can consciously filter out good ideas from bullshit (to some extent). What you might not realize, though, is that your current values and self-image are largely the product of the seeds of ideas that were planted when you were young and vulnerable.

We naturally assume that our beliefs must exist for good reason. We have to trust our own mind. Unfortunately, because of this trust, we have difficulty accepting that many of our ideas about ourselves and the world are totally illogical, toxic beliefs that we take ownership of simply because we had those ideas planted in our mindsets at a young age.

Say you don't think you're good looking enough to date attractive women. To you, this seems like a logical belief. You can clearly see that girls don't find you attractive; you can see all around you that it's mostly the good-looking guys that get attractive women. You know for a fact that you're not attractive to these women because they don't even give you the time of day. If you were able to get an attractive girlfriend, you'd obviously have one by now.

What you don't realize is that this belief really stems from your childhood. Maybe people teased you about your appearance, maybe you saw in films that the hot movie star ends up with the hot actress. One way or another, you unconsciously absorbed the cultural belief that physical attractiveness was necessary to date attractive women, and that you aren't good enough by this measure.

This idea that you picked up at a young age was like a seed that grew into a patch of weeds in your belief system. It's incredibly difficult to let go of the mindsets you picked up in your formative years because to do so would be to choose to abandon the foundation that your identity has been built on. Even if the foundation is a house of cards, it's your house of cards, something you've nurtured for years (without ever consciously deciding to). Your belief that attractive women can't like you is now a fundamental part of your belief system.

This means that if you were to find counter-evidence, if for example an attractive girl were to flirt with you, it would feel like an attack on your identity. You would resist the idea, fight against it, self-sabotage in your interactions with that girl so that you can prove that you're right in your belief that attractive girls don't like you.

If you don't believe attractive women should find you attractive, you have a confirmation bias (without knowing it) that is constantly searching for evidence that reinforces this belief. You will only see evidence that reinforces your negative self-belief. For example, when a girl looks at you and then quickly looks away, you'll assume she was repulsed by you. She must have looked away to avoid the pain of looking at you for another second.

But another guy, who got the same exact reaction from a girl, would think she was too shy to hold eye contact. He will assume she wanted to talk to him and approach her. He will ask for her number. She might say no, she might say yes. But because he doesn't have a mindset that causes him to reject himself, he doesn't miss the countless opportunities that most guys do.

A negative mindset is the psychological equivalent of cancer. The host doesn't know it is destroying itself. Becoming aware of this is intrinsically difficult because you'd have to admit that a part of you isn't really you, but a cancer.

It is your responsibility to have the courage to notice your own negative thinking, to question your insecurities, and to doubt your own self-doubt.

If your body were to become aware that it had cancer, your immune system would easily snuff it out. The same is true for a negative mindset, awareness of your own self-destructive beliefs is the cure.

The False Assumption That Ruins Men's Dating Lives

Many men use what appears to be a sound strategy to attract a girl they like. They try to impress her, show her how cool they are, and subtly change their persona to emulate the badass guy who does well with women.

This strategy rests on a fundamental assumption. She shouldn't like you by default; therefore, you must do something to win her affections.

Case Study: How I Fucked Myself Over Without Knowing It

A few years ago, I went on several dates with a girl who I thought was way out of my league. On the third date, I made a romantic gesture to win her over. At the end of our date, I hesitated, and took a deep breath, before pulling out a bouquet of flowers from the trunk of my car. I said, "I thought you might like these" (thinking I was being smooth). There was a long, awkward pause. She said, "Oh that's really sweet, thank you. But I have to go now." She then briskly walked away from me and into her home. I never saw her again.

A few months later, a stunning girl I worked with asked me on a date. We went out five or six times, we went to the park, the library, got high together, and on one fateful night she suggested that we watch a movie at my place. I agreed.

We were matching the movie in my bed, and she started massaging me. She had me lie down and kneaded my entire body. Eventually, she had me turn over so that she was on top of me in a cowgirl position. At this moment, I said, "Let's get back to the movie." She gave up at this point and we ended up sleeping, fully clothed, side-by-side. The morning after, she said, "Well, that's not what I expected. See ya."

These are both stories of last dates because I had a fundamental assumption that women shouldn't be attracted to me. I was insecure enough that I didn't make a move even when a girl massaged my entire body. I still wasn't convinced she wanted me to make something happen, there was still room for doubt. So, I kept waiting for further proof of her interest. In hindsight, it's obvious these girls were attracted to me, but they needed me to have the courage to take a risk.

How to Change Your False Assumptions

Men with deep self-confidence fundamentally assume women find them attractive. This may seem narcissistic and delusional, but it's a useful delusion that leaves room for risk taking (and by extension, results). On the other hand, delusionally believing you're unattractive is negative in a way that leaves room only for self-sabotage. (As a side-note, expecting girls to be attracted to you doesn't mean that you can't take no for an answer, it means that you are willing to take the risks that could lead to a no.)

The first step to developing this positive narcissism is counterintuitive: you must confront the possibility that you have negative beliefs that are holding you back. Accepting the possibility that you have beliefs about your attractiveness that may be negatively affecting your actions and results is difficult. But once you do, the problem finally becomes something you can control, and therefore, overcome.

The only way out is through. To change your beliefs, you must proactively take risks that normally only a man who assumes he is fundamentally attractive to women would take. This means putting yourself directly at risk for rejection by women (leaning in for the kiss, asking for the number, attempting the pull).

This is the first crucial step, yet most men never take it because their beliefs about their lack of attractiveness feel so real. If you think that you don't have enough money, the right body, or the right personality type to attract women, it's easy to see this perceived disadvantage as an insurmountable obstacle (women aren't going to start making moves on you anytime soon after all). By default, you will maintain your negative beliefs about yourself indefinitely.

You can easily shoot yourself in the foot when you have opportunities with women if you don't believe you are fundamentally attractive (like I did in the above anecdotes). Then, you will reinforce those beliefs because you didn't end up getting the girl. You will interpret these missed opportunities as further evidence that you are in fact correct in your self-evaluation that you are not sexually desirable to attractive women. It's a nasty self-fulfilling prophecy that happens outside of our conscious awareness.

The Power of Doubt

In your dating life (or any part of your social life), there is a sort of breadcrumb trail of neurotic and insecure emotions that you can follow. Your negative emotions feel like they're telling you to avoid something, but in reality, they're telling you exactly what you need to do. This means that if the notion of going out to meet women on a regular basis provokes anxiety, then do it: if getting rejected frightens you, then ask women out: pain points to the way forward.

The hardest part of this process is admitting that you're holding yourself back and avoiding taking the right actions. It's so easy to come up with excuses; you can tell yourself that you need to build more social skills before approaching more women, or that you need to wait to get your career handled, or you need to finish sculpting that six pack (don't get me wrong, those things definitely help, a lot, but they can easily turn into procrastination).

It's never going to be easy to admit that your emotional resistance is due to very real insecurities that you have. Understand this: changing your results is impossible without facing doubt and emotional resistance.

Wherever you experience resistance, you must question your assumptions about what that resistance means, this opens up room for you to doubt your current beliefs, which then entitles you to take risks that will disprove your negative mindset. Once you're aware of what's holding you back, your excuses lose their meaning. Therefore, you empower yourself to change.

The further you lean into your emotional resistance through risk-taking, the more you will find experiential proof that the resistance was based on unnecessary beliefs you had about yourself, not objective reality.

Within the context of success with women, the more you put yourself at a real risk of rejection (as a rule, to count as a rejection, she has to actually tell you no. Otherwise, you didn't really get rejected, you just rejected yourself), the more you will get evidence that a good number of women would very much enjoy the opportunity to fuck you.

Although you will find it hard to believe at first, over time, you will develop the fundamental assumption that women do find you attractive. This new assumption will entitle you to take more risks, which will then get you more results with women, which will then lead you to believe women find you even more sexually attractive. It's a powerful self-fulfilling prophecy that will take place outside of your conscious awareness.

By the way, if you get rejected and you feel hurt, these emotions aren't telling you that you're unattractive to women (no one is attractive to every woman), they are telling you that your self-esteem is based on how people react to you. As soon as you notice this, you can begin to let go of the pain that you create by caring too much. The pain associated with rejection, or not being likeable, is based on the meaning we give those concepts, not the events themselves.

With that said, go forth, chat up some stunners, get rejected a lot, succeed occasionally; and in so doing let go of and replace the unnecessary beliefs that were holding you back

Embrace Social Tension

We live among a generation of men who are so afraid of social confrontation that they avoid assertiveness like it's a plague. We've learned to value pleasantness over honesty and vulnerability. We keep it to ourselves when we disagree with someone, we keep it to ourselves when we want to say something controversial, and we keep it to ourselves when we have a crush because we are afraid of the social consequences of vulnerability.

We don't admit to ourselves that we do this, because to do so would be to accept a narrative that your ego is extremely fragile and easily damaged, which is a narrative that your ego is far too fragile to accept.

When attempting to become more aware of your own limiting beliefs, analyzing your thoughts is an important tool. It does have limitations, though. Your thoughts are not nearly as trustworthy as you'd like to believe.

Your conscious thoughts explain your emotions in a way that reinforces your self-concept. If you have a negative belief about yourself, your thoughts will be warped by that belief. It's important to question your thoughts, but the most effective tool for doing so is often through reading your emotions.

For example, if you believed that rejection wasn't a big deal, the following would be easy for you: Go to your college campus, a mall, or a bar and make new friends. Introduce yourself to at least three people.

For most people, this challenge isn't just hard, it triggers paralyzing anxiety. Hell, I tried this when I was eighteen. I still hadn't even kissed a girl so I gave myself a mission to approach women in hopes that I could get a date.

I went with a friend, we gave each other four hours to get some girls' numbers at our university campus. We were both nervous, but we figured with four hours we'd be able to make something happen.

As we walked around the campus, we saw girls we wanted to approach, but we always had an excuse:

"She's too tall."

"She's in a hurry."

"She's looking at her laptop."

"She looks like a lesbian." Etc.

Most of these excuses were bullshit, but they were compelling to us because they provided an opportunity to avoid our paralyzing fear of social tension and rejection.

After we spent two hours meandering around the campus, we had a realization: this wasn't going to work, we needed to change our approach. We decided to make our task easier by using a crutch. We absconded to a nearby corner store and bought two Four Lokos (which if you don't know, are 24 oz beer-like drinks with 12% alcohol content). This was enough to get us both drunk. We slammed down the drinks and felt reinvigorated due to the social lubrication.

We returned to campus midday, drunk, and… we repeated the same pattern (only this time we felt like idiots because we were drunk in the middle of the day). After two more hours of meandering around campus we walked home severely disappointed in ourselves.

We both avoided trying to meet women again for months. This should be an embarrassing anecdote that highlights an unusual social phobia that was shared by my friend and me. But it's not, because our social anxiety was in no way unusual. It's the norm. I've seen it time and time again, most guys become paralyzed with fear at the thought of saying hello to a stranger.

Logically, this behavior is absurd, there's nothing to be afraid of from approaching a girl. The worst-case scenario is that she isn't interested in talking to you and brushes you off. So what?

Our egos are a lot more fragile than we like to think (our ego has a strong desire to think that it isn't fragile). We give the simple act of meeting strangers tremendous meaning, thinking that if we're rejected we'll be humiliated or our reputation will be ruined.

The more desperately you avoid rejection, the more emotionally painful the thought of rejection will become. A man with deep inner confidence doesn't care about or avoid rejection; he has experienced it enough in the real world that it no longer means anything to him. He's okay with risking a socially tense moment by being assertive because he's been assertive enough times that he can't possibly buy into the delusion that boldness can lead to painful consequences.

A man of confidence is able to accept the fact that a stranger might be uninterested in meeting him, that his boss might not give him that raise, or that his crush might not like him back.

Because he's okay with the idea of rejection, it doesn't mean anything. Therefore, what for most people would be emotionally paralyzing is a non-event for him. He doesn't have an emotional need to be pleasing.

We don't protect ourselves from real social consequences; we protect ourselves from imagined social consequences. We do this so effectively that many people NEVER put themselves in a vulnerable position. The truth though, is that by protecting ourselves from rejection so desperately, we constantly reject ourselves.

If you're afraid a girl won't like you, you make her lose interest in you by playing it safe with her. If you're worried people won't like you enough, you make yourself less likeable by trying too hard to make people like you. Modern men put so much effort into keeping a pleasing mask on that they forget there's something better beneath that mask.

In college, I had a friend who gave zero fucks. What would have been extremely embarrassing for most people, was just a fun anecdote for him. Once, he walked up to his TA and asked her on a date in front of hundreds of students. He got brutally rejected, but the next day he told us the story while laughing about it.

I also had a TA I was attracted to. Unlike my friend, I wanted to ask her out in a pleasing way. I planned my big move throughout the semester. I considered asking her out during office hours, but I thought that would be too awkward for her. I told myself I'd wait until the last day of class and then ask her out when it ended.

After class, I sat in the hall and told myself I would wait for her to leave and then I'd ask her on a date (I didn't want to embarrass her in front of her students, after all). Of course, I hesitated and never ended up taking the risk. If I had asked her out, she probably would have rejected me, but so what?

I cared so much about whether or not I got rejected, that I rejected myself. I rationalized excuses that were profoundly stupid for an entire semester of college. If I had just stepped up, I would have had an anecdote about getting rejected that I could have laughed about later. Or, I might have gotten her number and ended up dating her. Now there's no way to know.

Since then, I made a rule for myself that has led to crazy (and sometimes embarrassing) stories. Whenever I get a gut feeling for a moment that I should approach a particular stranger, or ask someone out, or do anything that causes me to feel emotional resistance, I ask myself, "What would make the better memory?"

I don't always take action because of the question, but when I do, I never regret it. The answer to that question is almost always the best course of action to take.

Opportunity Versus Risk

Your 'reputation' is a fabrication of your biased assumption that people care about what you say or do. There is almost never any real social risk, yet we act like people will ostracize us if we do something that goes even slightly against the norm. Ironically, our efforts to protect our reputation make it impossible to have a good reputation in the first place.

We protect our reputation like a dragon protects gold (both are equally fictitious scenarios). Unless you commit a felony, pretty much anything you do will get brushed off by others as insignificant. We assume people think about us, because we spend most of our time doing exactly that. This assumption is totally inaccurate, your lover and your mother think about you; no one else gives a flying fuck what you say or do.

Men who are envied for their charisma or confidence are men who view what others see as risk, as opportunity. In dating, for example, most men are afraid of ruining their relationship with a female friend by asking her out. They worry that their friends will judge them if they get rejected by a girl at a bar. They worry that a girl might have a boyfriend who will beat them up for asking her out.

To this date, I've been rejected by hundreds of girls (mostly in bars and clubs). To my surprise no one has ever cared about these rejections but me. Furthermore, making a move on a girl I was friends with has never ruined the relationship, and paradoxically has even strengthened them. I've had a couple girls' boyfriends act a bit confrontational, but it's never led to anything close to a fight. The scenes of disastrous consequences due to social risk-taking we play out in our minds are entirely in our head. They never happen anywhere but in our egos.

I've tested this to the extreme to make a point to myself. I figured if there were one social faux pas that would have severe social consequences, it would be directly asking a woman I just met for sex. I approached several women and said, "Would you like to have sex with me?" And I was surprised by how pleasant the interactions were. A couple interactions were somewhat tense, but it wasn't a big deal. Shockingly, one girl even said, "I'm not sure. I don't know you well enough yet." (I'll leave the end of that story to your imagination).

I don't recommend doing this; it is an extremely awkward thing to say, but I found that it didn't affect my reputation at all. The consequences I had imagined for doing this were totally illusory.

Once you realize you don't have a reputation to ruin, you're free to actually build one. The only people who build a noteworthy reputation are those who are so carefree that they take the social risks others are too afraid to take. They are bold in a way that most aren't. Because of this, people pay more attention to them. They react to them.

Even if you are one of the few people who has a reputation, there's very little you can do to damage it. Even if you dance through the streets singing showtunes, people would, at most, find this bemusing. If a friend learned what you did, you could explain it was a joke or a social experiment and that would be that.

Ultimately, if you want to feel truly free in social situations, you must stop caring about your reputation. To accomplish this, you'll have to do those things that most people are too afraid to do. If, for example, you don't have the dating life you want, a great way to let go of caring too much would be to start approaching women. If possible, on a daily basis. You can do this at your college campus, a busy mall (or even a store like Target), bars, clubs, etc.

If you make a point to go out and face your social fears consistently, you will whittle away at your insecurities and prove to yourself that people don't care about what you do. That you aren't all that important. Once you realize other people don't give a fuck about you, you will be free to stop caring so much about what others think.

What exactly this will entail depends on your particular goals. If you want to improve your dating life, start asking strangers on dates, push yourself to attempt this regularly until you can do so comfortably. At first, the most you can do might be to go to a bar and say hi to people walking bye. That's okay, make a point to, over time, push yourself further. Once you're comfortable saying hi to people noncommittally, make a point to introduce yourself and start a conversation. Once you're comfortable starting conversations with strangers, start asking for dates.

If you are uncomfortable with social awkwardness, and feel like you can be too stiff. Take socially awkward actions that make you risk being judged by others. Dance in public, approach strangers and tell them jokes, go to your college campus and lay down on a busy sidewalk for a minute. Taking these actions will help you see that people aren't nearly as judgmental as you might think. This knowledge is extremely freeing.

This process may take some time, but the end results are worth the effort. My first attempts didn't go particularly well, and were very anxiety provoking. But, through putting myself through social discomfort repeatedly, not only did I become more confident, I also was able to improve my dating life drastically.

By taking the social risks that most people are too afraid to take, you will prove to yourself that the fears that held you back are meaningless. Through letting go of those fears you will become the rare person that other people not only pay attention to, but secretly envy.

Embrace Your Flaws

Acting like you don't care what people think is a symptom of caring way too much. Listening to criticism and social feedback, and thinking about it objectively, on the other hand, is a symptom of deep self-confidence.

This kind of honest scrutiny is difficult because it's when we feel the most fragile parts of our self-image are under attack that we get emotionally reactive. Those fragile points of vulnerability are the parts of our identity we defend most vigorously. The flaws you need to become aware of most are those that are the hardest to accept because they don't fit into your self-concept. Accomplishing this is fundamentally challenging, but extremely powerful.

Not too long ago, my friends started to call me overly competitive. Instead of saying, "What makes you think that?" I would reply with an offhanded (and intentionally cocky) response like, "A god does not compete with mortals."

I was sarcastic so I could avoid confronting the issue. I didn't respond with an open mind when I got called out on a bad social habit, that deep down, I knew I needed to change. I dealt with my exposed insecurity by brushing it under the rug with sarcasm. Addressing this issue with an open mind was the only way to overcome my biggest insecurities, but I blinded myself to the possibility that it was even an issue.

Months after I had begun getting called out on my hyper-competitiveness, I finally saw my insecurities rear their ugly head. I was in a small college writing class, and one student was answering most of the discussion questions. His answers were well thought-out and added substantial value to the discussion. But I got frustrated, I told myself he was an attention whore and that he should let other people contribute more.

In reality, he wasn't an attention whore. Most of the other students didn't even have something to contribute. I wasn't frustrated because he was hungry for attention, I was frustrated because I was hungry for attention. I saw the class as a social competition, and he was winning. I had an emotional need to be the 'main guy' in the class. I was jealous that someone else was charismatic, engaging, and intelligent. I was butthurt by the fact that he was offering more to the discussion than I was.

Until I realized what I was doing in that class, all the emotions I felt and decisions I made because of my machismo-infused competitiveness went completely unnoticed by me.

Beforehand, when people complained that I was too competitive, I consciously assumed they were jealous of me in some way (the irony is that even my thinking about my competitiveness was competitive without my awareness).

Blindspots to our own flaws are completely natural, and you can't expect to be so perfectly aware that you have a totally accurate self-image. However, it is possible to become more aware of your flaws and bad social habits, but it requires a counterintuitive approach. Remember that when you feel uncomfortable, the dialogue you tell yourself cannot be trusted because criticism and self-doubt put your ego on defense. Unfortunately, the voice in your head prioritizes the protection of your current self-image over open-minded self-reflection.

Instead, listen to your emotions. Whatever makes you emotionally reactive can become a goldmine for personal growth. When an interaction makes you angry, anxious, jealous, etc., that's when you can be sure you have insecure self-beliefs that you are not consciously aware of. Listen to your emotions much more closely than to the voice in your head.

Admit to yourself that the fact you are upset is telling you something that you probably don't want to hear. Once you come from this vulnerable, open-minded starting point, then and only then, you can start to accurately analyze what is causing you to feel emotional discomfort.

This process is difficult in a culture that teaches people to place blame on everyone but themselves. However, when you start assuming responsibility for your emotional reactions to people, situations, and criticism, you can accurately root out the instances when you are (at least partially) at fault. There are instances in which your emotional reactivity is warranted, but usually, emotional discomfort is indicative of something you should be working on internally.

What frustrates us about others tends to be what we're afraid of in ourselves. If you hate men who regularly sleep with girls on the first date, most likely you're either secretly jealous and unable to admit this to yourself, or you think that what he's doing is disrespectful and you're afraid that you're capable of acting the same way if you're not careful. Either way, this is saying a lot about your values and your insecurities, and very little about the other person.

I have a friend who is extremely uncomfortable around anyone who's a bit socially awkward. He will complain about how weird some guys are and treat them like shit. In his mind, this treatment is fair; these socially awkward people deserve to be treated poorly because they're awkward. But what he doesn't admit to himself is that he is terrified of being socially awkward himself. These people 'trigger' him not because they're socially awkward, but because he's afraid of the possibility that he might be socially awkward too.

This is an example of what famed psychologist Carl Jung calls the shadow. The shadow is all of the pieces of our identity (or ego) that we keep hidden from ourselves. My friend is so terrified of being awkward, that he will not do anything that makes him feel vulnerable. In fact, he will regularly dare me to pull unusual stunts in public when we go out, like approaching a girl with an awkward pickup line (Is it hot in here? Or is that just the holy spirit burning inside of you?).

Numerous times after completing my challenge, I gave him a similar task and he always became visibly nervous and refuses to do it. To this day, he hasn't done a single thing that he thought was socially uncalibrated, even when offered money to do so as a bet.

His fear of being socially awkward is understandable (yet irrational), but what makes it so powerful is that he won't admit to himself that he has this fear. The only way he can come to terms with his own insecurities is by assuming that his emotional discomfort is reflective of his own flaws instead of placing the blame on others.

Realizations likes this catalyze significant change, yet this is always emotionally challenging. It requires a mindset shift towards your own negative emotions. You must realize that emotional resistance isn't something to avoid, but something to lean into and learn from. Negative emotions aren't bad, they're revealing a point of vulnerability in your own self-concept.

Negative emotions are signposts for your own neurotic and insecure beliefs, and they're screaming at you to become aware of this to make a change. As soon as you see these emotions as signals, as opportunities for growth, they transform from something to be avoided, to something to be sought out purposefully.

On Surrender

Any state of social discomfort, whether it be anxiety, stress, or frustration, is a state of resistance. Negative emotions are so uncomfortable because they make you feel like you're not in control. When in such a state, you want to regain power over your emotions. Struggling against these feelings only gives them more charge. The act of fighting your emotions is what gives them so much power over you. This is a totally normal response, but it doesn't work. The solution to social discomfort is extremely counterintuitive. Surrender to it.

The process is similar to exercise. At first, exercise is extremely uncomfortable, you are intentionally putting yourself through physical pain to grow stronger. When new to working out, you will feel an emotional resistance to going to the gym. The pain of working out is something you'll have a desire to avoid.

But continuously lean into the pain on purpose, and your response to that pain changes. Eventually, the pain and discomfort transforms into something that is enjoyable for its own sake. These feelings were subjective, and by consistently going to the gym you were training your brain to want to lean into the pain of exercise, and eventually you began to gain pleasure from it.

We have a habit of avoiding discomfort. It is like pulling on a rubber band, the harder you pull the more tension you create (until eventually it's too much and you snap by having a panic attack or emotional outburst). Instead, intentionally trying to intensify that discomfort diffuses the emotional tension. Once you embrace discomfort, it stops being uncomfortable. Whenever I feel social discomfort, I intentionally intensify it.

How do you do this? Through your conscious intention. Conscious intention sounds very woo-woo but it's actually well-grounded in experience. To understand what a conscious intention is, try to make your hands experience a tingling sensation (or to make them feel colder, or hotter).

If you do this with focus, you will notice the sensations in your hand do indeed change in the way you intended them to.

That's all conscious intention is; it is your mental desire to feel something. When you feel social discomfort (uncomfortable emotions or physical sensations), intend to make that discomfort more intense. You will find that the intensity does in fact increase. At first, this will be challenging.

This practice is sending your brain the message that whatever emotion or sensation it is you are intensifying is not a bad emotion. It is not an emotion that you need to avoid, and therefore that feeling stops being stressful. You will still experience similar feelings in the future, but they will stop triggering psychological resistance.

We all develop our own responses to discomfort, the emotions and sensations you will experience are unique to you. Simply begin to focus on them, intensify them, and they will, over time, have less and less power over you.

I've made this into a meditative practice. The most well-known meditation in the west, mindfulness meditation, is a practice of bringing awareness to your thoughts. Instead, this is a pain meditation. I focus on my negative sensations and emotions, and intentionally intensify them. I sit down for ten minutes, scan my body, and wherever I feel discomfort (emotion or sensation), I focus on that discomfort and use my conscious intention to magnify that feeling.

This retrains my body to embrace difficult emotions the same way exercise retrains the body to embrace physical pain.

You won't stop having negative emotions through doing this, but your relationship with those negative emotions will qualitatively change. They will no longer have power over you, they will still affect you, but they won't have a negative charge.

Your discomfort exists for a reason, and once you stop resisting it, discomfort can serve its real purpose, which is to guide you towards actions you ought to take. When you feel butterflies in your stomach, instead of fighting the discomfort, you will see it as a sign that you need to talk to that girl. When you feel afraid to speak up, you'll see that fear as a call to action, not something to struggle against. When you feel uncomfortable at the thought of going out, you will no longer cope with that discomfort by numbing yourself with social media; instead you will feel compelled to leave your cave and meet people in the real world.

Kill Complaint

"Never complain, never explain."- Benjamin Disraeli

Everyone knows complaining is a toxic habit, yet it's a favorite American pastime. Complaining is never a winning strategy; maybe you'll get a momentary hit of self-righteousness from it, you might get off by victimizing yourself, but that's the only benefit.

The high you get from complaining is an addictive form of self-validation that reinforces negative behaviors, negative emotions, and negative beliefs. When you complain, you're passing the blame onto someone else: you're deferring responsibility for your problems. In so doing, you're reinforcing a mindset that says external circumstances have power over you.

Whenever you complain, you are subtly telling yourself, "My life is being harmed because of X," and that X is always something external, meaning you're telling yourself that the quality of your life is being detrimentally affected by something that you have no control over.

A small man has small problems, a powerful man focuses on problems that are larger than himself. When you let the minutia of everyday problems affect you, you are shrinking your world to match the size of your problems. You are stripping yourself of power by letting small things that are ultimately unimportant affect you. A problem isn't worthy of getting emotionally invested in unless you would look back 10 years from now and regret not doing more about it.

Even for these problems, though, complaint isn't the solution.

Without Complaint, There Is Only Action

Imagine that your mother is pushing you into a career that you've realized isn't something you're passionate about. Now you've invested a couple years of your college education and a lot of money into that career path. To blow off steam, you regularly complain to your friends about how domineering she was. What is complaining accomplishing here?

Complaining is giving you an excuse to feel self-righteously upset in place of taking action. You are rationalizing to yourself and your friends that you are trapped, and in so doing, you're making yourself feel trapped. But if you don't complain, that emotional energy can only go towards solving your problem.

Our propensity for complaint is one of our biggest blind spots to ourselves. No one self identifies as a complainer (and if you are aware that you are complaining you almost certainly think that your complaints are about real, significant problems. Of course, even if your complaints are about real, significant problems, there's no reason to give those problems power over you). I'm not suggesting you ignore your problems, I'm suggesting you don't waste your time or energy talking about them.

Accept the possibility that you may have a habit of complaining. You can get quantifiable proof one way or the other by downloading a click counter app on your smartphone. For three days, look for any complaining you might be doing in your conversations, and add a point to the app whenever you do so (if you're not sure whether something is a complaint, it probably is). Once you've done this for a few days, you will have a good idea of whether or not you complain, and if you do, it will now be possible to catch yourself in the future. It will be easy to stop doing it because the feeling of complaining will be repulsive when you're aware of what you're doing.

Eliminating complaint will not only improve your social relationships directly because complaining is always unattractive, but also indirectly, because complaining is a major source of self-inflicted damage to our self-image.

An Outward Focus

When we focus on ourselves, we prevent ourselves from experiencing the world outside of our own head. Living in your head is detrimental. Too often, the thoughts in your head are less like a cheerleader squad, and more like a team of football players giving you a swirly. The ability to connect with others starts with the ability to disconnect from yourself. To make a positive impression on others, stop thinking about how charming you're being (or not being) and stop analyzing what people are thinking about you. Instead, start showing curiosity towards other people.

When we feel insecure around others we waste our mental energy attempting to extrapolate what they're thinking about us. We worry about the negative impression we might be making and think about how we can improve that impression.

To make a great impression, to make people like you, you must be indifferent to what they think of you, and instead focus your attention on them. Not only will this make people like you more, but it takes the weight of self-judgment off your shoulders. You can only be insecure when you're thinking about yourself.

Focus outwardly. A great example of this can be seen in the debates between Bill Clinton and George H.W. Bush. Regardless of political affiliation, most people agreed that Clinton was the more charismatic candidate. In one question, the difference between the two men was made

clear.

When a woman asked about whether a wealthy man like himself could really understand the poor, George H.W. Bush was defensive and made the question about him instead of the impoverished Americans the questions was really about.

When Bill Clinton answered the same question, all his attention focused on the woman who asked it, and he related everything he said back to her. He was curious about her situation rather than making the question about him.

When speaking of Bill Clinton many people mention that he made them feel like they were the only person in the room when talking to him. His external focus is captivating whereas Bush's self-focus is anti-magnetic.

To practice this shift, understand that human interactions are rich with potential insights. See this as a sort of game. Make interactions with people an opportunity to understand their motives and beliefs.

Wonder what people are trying to accomplish with their words, why they're saying what they're saying, why their body language is tense or loose, or why they have a particular social habit. The primary goal of this is to shift your focus off yourself and on to the people you are interacting with. Doing so will not only engage you more in social interactions, but it will also make you more engaging. When you do this, your interactions stop being opportunities for you to focus on your own problems, and instead become opportunities to connect with others and enter a state of curiosity.

Not only will this make people like and respect you more because you are showing genuine interest in them, but it will also help you understand how people think, and with that understanding comes power.

One of the most important lessons you will learn through this practice is the extent of most peoples' insecurities and self-doubt. You will see that people are embarrassed about their imperfections, and they put tremendous effort into trying to hide those imperfections from others. The more you notice other people's imperfections, the less seriously you will need to take your own.

It's important to distinguish that you're not doing this to judge others, but to understand them. You will notice people have habits that are not serving them, but this doesn't mean you're superior to them, it's just evidence of your shared humanity. Truly open-minded curiosity allows you to analyze people empathetically instead of through a filter of emotional defensiveness. This allows you to connect with them deeply and enjoy interacting with them far more than you would otherwise.

Conclusion

It's Not All About You

The root cause of most of our social difficulties is our egoistic tendency to over-dramatize our own importance. We try to solve these difficulties with the same type of thinking that caused them, and in so doing, when we try to build confidence we often end up making ourselves more insecure. The more we analyze our flaws and try to fix them, the more attention we pay to our flaws, and therefore, the more power we give to them. This doesn't work because it can't work. It's an intrinsically flawed strategy. You can't become more charismatic by thinking about yourself more (my body language, my voice, what I'm saying), doing this only makes you more insecure and defensive.

Don't take the notion of caring less to mean that what makes people socially attractive is an indifference to others, it isn't. What makes people socially attractive is an ability to be engaged with others instead of making everything about themselves.

Other people, just like you, care mostly about themselves. By taking your focus off of yourself, you can give people the attention they want, and in so doing you will become both more confident and charismatic, not only because you are less insecure, but also because you will give people what they want most, to really be heard.

Make a habit of challenging your own doubts and insecurities. Make a habit of seeking out your own blind spots, and facing your social fears. Do this and the external results that most others try to force by putting on a mask and projecting a false image, will come to you naturally. You will be smart, capable, and most importantly, free in all the ways most people are not.

About the Author

Avery Hayden is the author of Zero Fucks Given, The Trial: Transform Your Dating Life in Eight Weeks, among others. He lives in Arizona where he studied psychology and creative writing at the University of Arizona.

Because of his struggles with anxiety, he has been obsessed with psychology and self-improvement for many years. He believes there is a need for more self-improvement with a solid scientific foundation.

You can find free articles by Avery at: https://redpilltheory.com

Other Books by Avery Hayden:

The Trial: Transform Your Dating Life In Eight Weeks

How to Conquer Social Anxiety: A Scientific, Step-By-Step Formula to Overcome Shyness, Break Free From Negative Thinking, and Unlock True Confidence

The Art and Science of Goal Completion

Printed in Great Britain
by Amazon